DATE DUE

SEP 14, 2006	

PRINTED IN U.S.A.

The United States

Alaska

Bob Italia
ABDO & Daughters

visit us at
www.abdopub.com

Published by Abdo & Daughters, 4940 Viking Drive, Suite 622, Edina, Minnesota 55435.
Copyright © 1998 by Abdo Consulting Group, Inc., Pentagon Tower, P.O. Box 36036,
Minneapolis, Minnesota 55435 USA. International copyrights reserved in all countries.
No part of this book may be reproduced in any form without written permission from the
publisher.

Printed in the United States.

Cover and Interior Photo credits: Peter Arnold, Inc., Natural Selection, Super Stock

Edited by Lori Kinstad Pupeza
Contributing editor Brooke Henderson
Special thanks to our Checkerboard Kids—John Hansen, Tyler Wagner, Stephanie
McKenna

All statistics taken from the 1990 census; The Rand McNally Discovery Atlas of The
United States. Other sources: Compton's Encyclopedia, 1997; *Alaska*, Heinrichs,
Children's Press, Chicago, 1989.

Library of Congress Cataloging-in-Publication Data

Italia, Bob, 1955-
     Alaska / Bob Italia.
     p.   cm. -- (The United States)
     Includes index.
     Summary: Examines the geography, history, natural resources, people, and
     culture of the largest state in the United States.
     ISBN 1-56239-855-5
     1. Alaska--Juvenile literature. [1. Alaska.] I. Title. II. Series: United States
     (Series)
     F904.3.I83   1998
     979.8--dc21   97-12013
                                        CIP
                                        AC

Contents

Welcome to Alaska

Alaska is the largest state in America, but not many people live there. It lies along the **Arctic** Circle, separated from the "Lower 48" states.

Inuits, **Aleuts**, Athabascans, Tlingit, and Haida were the first people to live in Alaska. Russians visited Alaska in 1648. More Europeans came to Alaska in the early 1900s. In 1867, the United States bought Alaska from Russia.

Gold was found in Nome in 1899. The United States built military bases in the 1940s. Alaska became a state in 1959. In 1968, oil and **natural gas** were found in northern Alaska. Oil companies began pumping oil out of Alaska's ground in 1977.

The name Alaska comes from an Aleut word thought to mean "mainland" or "land that is not an island."

Today, Alaska still pumps oil out of the ground for the United States. It is also becoming a favorite tourist spot, thanks to its rugged beauty.

A mountain reflection on a pond.

Fast Facts

ALASKA

Capital
Juneau (26,751 people)
Area
570,833 square miles
(1,478,451 sq km)
Population
551,947 people
Rank: 49th
Statehood
January 3, 1959
(49th state admitted)
Principal river
Yukon River
Highest point
Mount McKinley; 20,320 feet
(6,194 m)
Largest city
Anchorage (226,338 people)
Motto
North to the future
Song
"Alaska's Flag"
Famous People
Vitus Bering, Carl Eielson,
Joe Juneau, William H. Seward

*S*tate Flag

*F*orget-Me-Not

*W*illow Ptarmigan

*S*itka Spruce

About Alaska

The Last Frontier State

AK

Alaska's abbreviation

Detail area

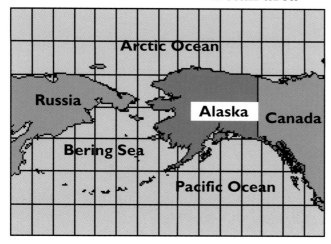

Borders: west (Bering Sea), north (Arctic Ocean), east (Canada), south (Pacific Ocean)

Nature's Treasures

Alaska has huge areas of natural beauty. There are snowcapped mountains, giant **glaciers**, dense forests, and rolling **tundra**.

Small plants such as lichens, mosses, flowering plants, and grasses grow in the tundra. Tundra is found on higher mountain slopes and covers most of western Alaska and all of **Arctic** Alaska.

Other parts of the state are covered by forests of hemlock, Sitka spruce, black and white spruce, birch, aspen, and larch. Flowers like asters, forget-me-nots, violets, arctic daisies, and mountain laurels grow wild in Alaska.

Alaskan wildlife includes many big animals. Deer and bear wander through the southern part of the state. Arctic Alaska has polar bears, caribou, and arctic foxes.

Alaska also has herds of moose, caribou, reindeer, musk-oxen, mountain goats, and sheep. Trout, salmon, and other fish swim in Alaska's streams. Salmon, halibut, cod, herring, pollack, shrimp, clams, crabs, and whales are found along the coast.

The most important **minerals** in Alaska are oil and **natural gas**. They are found in great amounts in the **Arctic** region. Gold can be found on the Seward Peninsula and in the Alaska Panhandle. Alaska also has one of North America's largest coal **deposits**.

The Trans-Alaska Pipeline carries oil across Alaska.

Beginnings

Native Americans lived all over Alaska when the first settlers of Alaska came from Asia across the Bering land bridge.

In 1728, the Danish sailor Vitus Bering visited and named St. Lawrence Island. People returned to Russia with sea otter furs from Alaska. Soon Russians were trapping in the **Aleutian** Islands. Several **settlements** were built.

Most of Alaska's **boundaries** were set by Russia, Great Britain, and the United States. U.S. secretary of state William H. Seward bought Alaska in 1867 for $7.2 million. (That's about two cents for an acre.) Alaska was called "Seward's Folly" because many people thought the land was useless.

In 1899, gold was found on the beach at Nome. Soon, people rushed to Alaska to dig for gold. By 1900, about

10,000 gold seekers were in Nome.

Juneau was made the capital of Alaska in 1900. In 1912, Alaska became a United States territory. In 1923, the Alaska Railroad, running from Seward to Fairbanks, was finished.

Oil was found in 1957 in the Kenai Peninsula-Cook Inlet region. On January 3, 1959, Alaska became the 49th state. Its first governor was William A. Egan.

Oil and **natural gas** were found near Prudhoe Bay in 1968. Oil was sent by pipeline from northern Alaska to the ice-free **port** of Valdez. There, the oil would be put on big ships called tankers. The Trans-Alaska Pipeline was finished in 1977.

The money made from oil helped everyone in the state. But in March 1989, the supertanker Exxon Valdez spilled 11 million gallons (41.6 million liters) of oil into Prince William Sound off Valdez. This disaster ruined many miles of coastline and killed a lot of wildlife.

B.C. to 1800

The First Settlements

 10,000 to 3,000 years ago the first settlers came to the area from Asia across the Bering land bridge.

 1728: Vitus Bering visits and names the area St. Lawrence Island.

 1784: The Russians make the first non-Native American settlement.

Alaska

B.C. to 1800

1800 to 1923

U.S. Purchases Alaska

 1867: U.S. Secretary of State William Seward purchases Alaska from Russia.

 1899: Gold is found in Nome; the gold rush begins.

 1912: The territory of Alaska is created.

 1923: The Alaskan Railroad is completed.

14

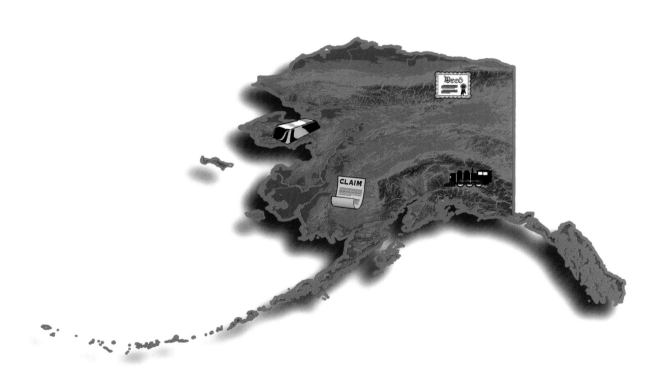

1957 to Present

Statehood and Beyond

 1957: Oil is discovered on Kenai Peninsula.

 1959: Alaska becomes the 49th state.

 1964: Alaska is devastated by an earthquake.

 1977: The Alaskan Pipeline is completed.

 1989: Exxon Valdez spills more than 240,000 barrels of oil into Prince William Sound.

Alaska
1957 to Present

Alaska's People

Alaska is one of the least **populated** states. About 16 percent of Alaska's population are **Native Americans**, **Inuits**, and **Aleuts**. Most of these people live in the north and east. They feed themselves and make money by catching fish and sea **mammals**, and by herding reindeer.

The largest Native American Nation are the Athabascan-speaking Native Americans. They live in central Alaska. The Haida, Tlingit, and Tsimshian live in the southeast part of the state. Aleutians live on the Alaska Peninsula and on the Aleutian and Shumagin islands.

William Egan was born in 1914 in Valdez. He was a member of the House of Representatives, was a Senator, and became the first governor of Alaska in 1959.

Susan Butcher moved to Alaska in 1975. In 1986, she won the famous Iditarod Sled Dog Race and set a record time. In 1987, she broke her own record. In 1988, she became the first person to win three years in a row.

Inuit children in Alaska.

Splendid Cities

There are seven main cities in Alaska: Anchorage, Fairbanks, Juneau, Kenai, Ketchikan, Sitka, and Kodiak.

Anchorage is the largest city. It is also a busy **port**. Anchorage sends oil ships year-round. Alaska Pacific University and the University of Alaska at Anchorage are here. The city had Alaska's first radio station and first television stations.

Fairbank's main **industries** include mining and lumbering. Fort Wainwright and Eielson Air Force Base are nearby. The capital of Alaska is Juneau.

Fairbanks

Anchorage

Juneau

Kenai

Sitka

Ketchikan

Kodiak

It is the second largest city in land area in the United States. Sitka, Alaska, is the biggest. Juneau has an ice-free harbor, an airport, and a seaplane base.

Juneau, Alaska

Alaska's Land

Alaska has four different areas. The Pacific mountains are in the south. In the middle region hills spread across the land. The Brooks Range, which is the northern part of the Rocky Mountains, is in the northern part of Alaska. The **Arctic** coastal plain, or North Slope, sits on the very north tip of the state.

The main river in Alaska is the Yukon. It flows westward across the central part of the state and empties into the Bering Sea. Other major rivers in the state are the Kuskokwim, the Kobuk, and the Noatak. Each river flows into a different body of water.

Alaska has many lakes. The largest is Iliamna Lake in the south. Several big lakes, such as Becharof Lake, Naknek Lake, and Kukaklek Lake, are on the Alaska Peninsula.

The northern coast of Alaska.

Alaska at Play

Alaska's beautiful scenery brings thousands of tourists. National Park Service land—most of it set aside in 1978—covers about 51 million acres. People hike and ski at Mount McKinley, Gates of the **Arctic**, Glacier Bay, and many other national parks and preserves.

One historic site in Alaska is at a place where gold was found, the Klondike Gold Rush National Historical Park. Sitka National Historical Park has the site of the 1804 battle where the Tlingits were defeated by Russian settlers.

Alaska's museums display native traditions and history. There are many museums in Alaska that show the history of the people of Alaska. Anchorage has a museum of fine arts and native crafts.

Dog sled racing is a popular sport in Alaska. People

race across the snow in sleds that are pulled by a team of dogs. The strong dogs have thick fur so they don't get cold.

Dog sled racing in Anchorage, Alaska.

Alaska at Work

Alaskans work to make available much of the oil used in the United States. Lumbering, fishing, and tourism are also important **industries**.

Farmers produce milk, eggs, hay, and potatoes. The state has just a few hundred farms. Reindeer are raised in Alaska. Some sheep and cattle are raised, and Alaska has thousands of horses. Southeastern Alaska has an important logging and paper-pulp industry. Alaskans also work at small lumber mills in the Fairbanks and Anchorage areas.

Alaska has an important fishing industry, which produces more fish than all other states. Salmon is the biggest catch.

Hunting is an important industry in Alaska. The fur and skin from moose, caribou, seals, and whales bring in a lot of money for Alaskans.

Oil is the leading **mineral** produced in Alaska. Oil is transported by the 800 mile long (1,287 km long) Trans-Alaska Pipeline to Valdez. There, the oil is put on big ships called tankers.

Alaska has a small **manufacturing industry**. The main products are fish, paper, lumber, and oil.

Fishing is big business in Alaska.

Fun Facts

•The state's highest peak is Mount McKinley at 20,320 feet (6,194 m). It is also the highest point in North America.

•Alaska contains the northernmost land point of the United States—Point Barrow.

•The western tip of the Seward Peninsula of Alaska is only about 50 miles (80 km) from the Russian mainland.

•Alaska has 6,639 miles (10,684 km) of coastline. Most of Alaska's territory is owned by the federal government.

•Alaska is known as the "Land of the Midnight Sun." That is because around the height of summer, the sun barely sets before it rises again. So even at night time it is light outside. In the middle of winter, the sun barely rises before it sets again, which means that it's dark outside all day long.

Mount McKinley, Alaska

Glossary

Aleuts: people of the Aleutian and Shumagin islands in western Alaska.

Arctic: at or near the North Pole.

Boundary: a border.

Deposit: a mass of some mineral or rock in the ground.

Glacier: a large mass of ice made from the snow on high ground that moves very slowly down a mountain or along a valley.

Industry: any form of business.

Inuit: a group of Native Americans that live in Alaska, the American Eskimo people of Alaska.

Mammal: any warm-blooded animal with a backbone and hair.

Manufacturing: to make a lot of something in large numbers.

Mineral: something that is mined or dug out of the earth.

Natural gas: a gas formed naturally in the earth.

Native Americans: the first people to live in America.

Populated: lived in by people.

Population: the people of a city, country, or district.

Port: a harbor; a place where ships can be sheltered from storms or where they can load and unload goods.

Settlement: a group of people who set up an area to live in a new country.

Tundra: a large, flat, treeless land in the arctic regions.

Internet Sites

Alaska Guide
http://www.alaskaguide.com
Here you will find all you need to know to travel in one of the world's most beautiful places. Alaska is the land of the Midnight Sun. Rich in culture, from its people to the majestic Mt. McKinley (Denali National Park) where caribou and bear roam the wide open spaces.

See Alaska Online
http://www.alaskanet.com
Welcome to Alaska. Sit back and experience the Last Frontier as you never have . . . right from your desktop.

These sites are subject to change. Go to your favorite search engine and type in Alaska for more sites.

PASS IT ON

Tell Others Something Special About Your State

To educate readers around the country, pass on interesting tips, places to see, history, and little unknown facts about the state you live in. We want to hear from you!

To get posted on ABDO & Daughters website E-mail us at "mystate@abdopub.com"

Index